BIONIC LIMBS

BY HOLLY DUHIG

Gareth Stevens
PUBLISHING

Please visit our website, **www.garethstevens.com**.
For a free color catalog of all our high-quality books,
call toll free 1-800-542-2595 or fax 1-877-542-2596.

Cataloging-in-Publication Data
Names: Duhig, Holly.
Title: Bionic limbs / Holly Duhig.
Description: New York : Gareth Stevens Publishing, 2018. |
    Series: Science fiction to science fact | Includes index.
Identifiers: ISBN 9781538214527 (pbk.) | ISBN 9781538213803
    (library bound) | ISBN 9781538214534 (6 pack)
Subjects: LCSH: Bionics--Juvenile literature. | Prosthesis--
    Juvenile literature.
Classification: LCC Q320.5 D84 2018 | DDC 617.9--dc23

Published in 2018 by
Gareth Stevens Publishing
111 East 14th Street, Suite 349
New York, NY 10003

Written by: Holly Duhig
Edited by: John Wood
Designed by: Matt Rumbelow

Photo credits: Abbreviations: l-left, r-right, b-bottom, t-top, c-center,
m-middle. With thanks to Getty Images, Thinkstock Photo and
iStockphoto. Cover: bg – Willyam Bradberry, 2 – Sarah Holmlund, 4l
– Maxx-Studio, 4r – fotoslaz, 5 – wax, 6 – ostill, 7tr – Ociacia, 7b –
Ase, 8t – photopixel, 8b – Sebastian Kaulitzki, 9 – whitehoune, 10t –
ociacia, 10b – Billion Photos, 11l – ESB Professional, 11r – Value Vitaly,
12bg – Ericsmandes, 12m – adike, 13 – Dmitry Lobanov, 14t – William
Bradberry, 14m – Oksana Kuzmina, 14b – Sladic, 15bg – Dragon
Images, 15m – martynowi.cz, 16 – WillyamBradberry, 17t – kudia, 17b
– Willyan Bradberry, 18t – belushi, 18b – fotoslaz, 19 – Sarah Holmlund,
20 – Elnur, 21t – rimon, 21m – Ahmet Misurligul, 21b – Kichigin, 22 –
Antonio Gulliem, 23t – Rost9, 23b – Elsa Hoffman, 24 – Ociacia, 25
– Neil Harbisson Cyborgist, 26t – Sergey Nivens, 26b – whiteMocca,
27m – Sashkin, 27b – sdecoret, 28 – gangis khan, 29t – Laremenko
Sergii, 29b – Ivan Smuk, 30 – Tatiana Shepeleva.

Printed in China
CPSIA compliance information: Batch CW18GS: For further information contact
Gareth Stevens, New York, New York at 1-800-542-2595.

SYSTEM
PROTECTION

LOGIN
PASSWORD

3.5

1.41

CONTENTS

Words that appear like this can be found in the glossary on page 31.

WHAT IS BIONICS?

Bionics is the science of making technology that acts like real body parts. The word "bionics" is a combination of biology and electronics. An electronic arm that acts like a human arm is a bionic arm. Bionics is all about technology that can make our bodies faster, stronger, and smarter.

It might sound like a science of the future but, in reality, bionic technology has been around for ages. Hearing aids are an example of bionic technology for your ears that can help you hear better. Ever since the science of bionics really started taking off, scientists and engineers have been working hard to make better, more advanced bionic body parts. In fact, the future of bionics now lies in something very exciting indeed: bionic limbs.

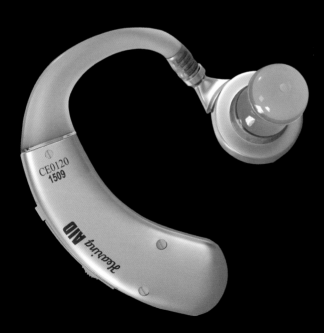

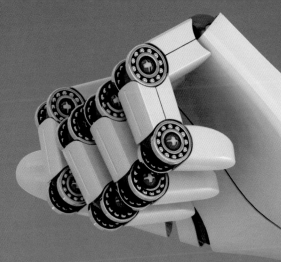

WHAT ARE BIONIC LIMBS?

Your limbs are your arms, legs, hands, and feet. Bionic limbs are mechanical versions of these. Bionic limbs can be used to help people who were born without one or more of their limbs or have had them amputated.

PROSTHETICS

Prosthetic limbs are human-made, or artificial, replacements of missing body parts. People who have had limbs amputated often use prosthetics. When you think of missing limbs, you might imagine peg-legged pirates with hooks for hands. This is because wooden legs and metal hooks were types of early prosthetics. Luckily prosthetic limbs have come a long way since then! Bionic limbs are the latest type of prosthetic technology.

BIONICS: THE FANTASY

People have always dreamed of being able to improve their bodies with new technology. Imagine being able to lift up cars and buses with a bionic arm that gives you superstrength. Or becoming a bionic basketball champion with arms and legs that can stretch as far as you need them to. Arms and legs are easily broken. If you've ever broken a bone, you know how painful it can be! Bionic limbs, however, can be easily replaced or fixed. You can see the appeal. Being half-human, half-machine could give us superhuman abilities. But if you had the chance to become part robot, would you take it?

Many authors and moviemakers have imagined a future where humans and machines are one and the same. In the world of science fiction, robotic body parts are sometimes called "cybernetic enhancements." There are many stories of people getting carried away with technology and turning themselves into "cyborgs." A cyborg (or "cybernetic organism") is someone who has both human and bionic body parts.

In the television show *Doctor Who*, the Cybermen are an alien race of cyborgs. They are the villains that the Doctor just can't shake. They deleted their emotions and turned themselves into a cold, hard, metal army in order to live forever. Would you become a mixture of human and robot parts if it meant living forever?

In reality, scientists are far from building an army of cyborgs, but even so, the future of bionic body parts might not be as far away as you think. In fact, scientists are already making real-life bionic limbs, some of which can even be controlled by our minds!

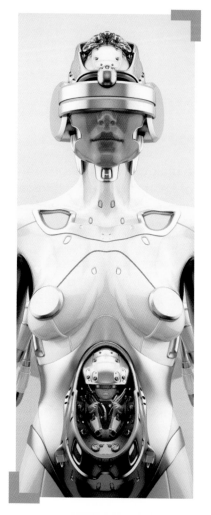

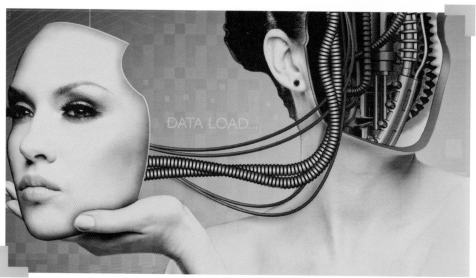

DATA LOAD...

BIONIC LIMBS: MOVEMENT AND FEELING

BIONIC AND BIOLOGICAL

A biological limb is one that is made of flesh and bone, whereas a bionic limb is made of mechanical parts. In order to make a bionic limb move, scientists must first understand how our bodies make biological limbs move. Most of us are lucky enough to be able to move our arms and legs whenever we want without even thinking about it. If you were to accidentally touch a hot stove, you would be able to pull your arm back straight away without even having to think about it. This might seem automatic to you, but your body is actually very busy making this movement happen.

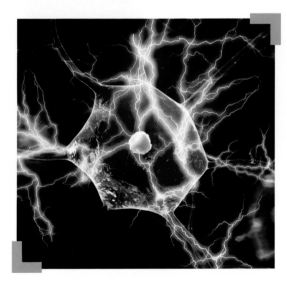

Your body is packed full of cells called nerves which make up your nervous system. Your nervous system is responsible for your movement and sense of touch. When you touch a hot stove, nerves in your fingers send a message to your brain to let it know you are in pain. Your brain then sends a message back to the muscles in your fingers to tell them to pull away from the thing that's hurting them.

But how are these messages sent? Well, just like a machine, your body uses electricity. The messages are actually sent to and from your brain in the form of tiny **impulses** of electricity. These impulses are carried by nerve cells called motor neurons. Movement feels automatic because motor neurons carry these impulses at 250 miles per hour (400 km/h)!

Sending a message from your brain to one of your limbs is a lot like turning on an electric light. When you flick a light switch, electricity is sent through wires to a lightbulb to turn it on. Nerves are like the wires of our nervous system.

YOU HAVE OVER 7,000 NERVE ENDINGS IN EACH FOOT.

MIND-CONTROLLED BIONIC LIMBS

If we are not that different from machines after all, perhaps becoming part robot might be easier than we think. If our bodies use electricity biologically, could we use it to power a robot arm as well?

This is what scientists have been scratching their heads over for quite some time. So far, prosthetics haven't been very good at moving on their own. Some prosthetic arms are able to copy the movements of the opposite, real arm. But this isn't very useful. In everyday life, we need to use both arms separately. Just think about how you eat your dinner — you use a fork with one hand and a knife with the other.

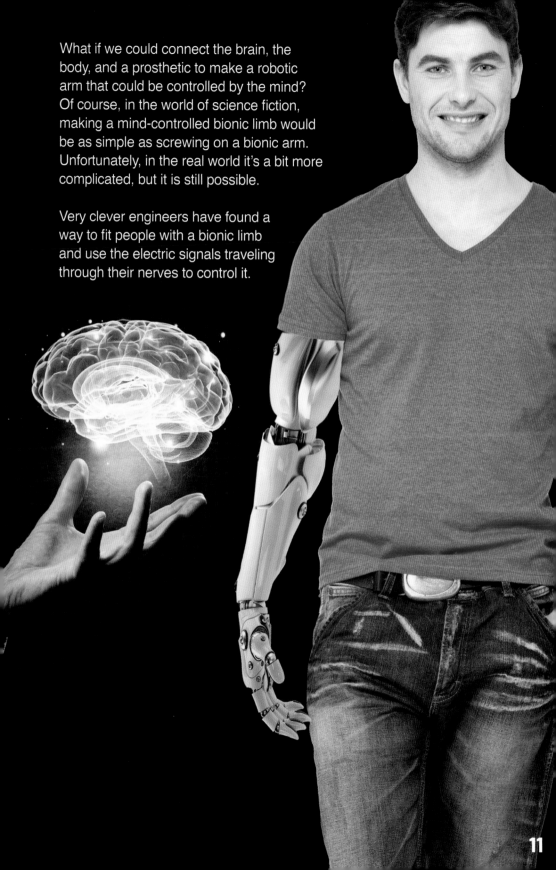

What if we could connect the brain, the body, and a prosthetic to make a robotic arm that could be controlled by the mind? Of course, in the world of science fiction, making a mind-controlled bionic limb would be as simple as screwing on a bionic arm. Unfortunately, in the real world it's a bit more complicated, but it is still possible.

Very clever engineers have found a way to fit people with a bionic limb and use the electric signals traveling through their nerves to control it.

WHO WOULD THIS HELP?

Many people have had one or more of their limbs amputated. When a limb is amputated, the nerves that connect it to the rest of the body are cut in two.

Even after a limb has been removed, the brain will still fire messages towards it. The brain gets very confused when these messages hit a dead end. This can cause something called phantom limb pain where people feel pain in the limb that's no longer there. The worst thing about phantom limb pain is that it can't be fully treated. A bionic limb that can be controlled by the brain could help ease this pain by giving the brain's messages somewhere to go.

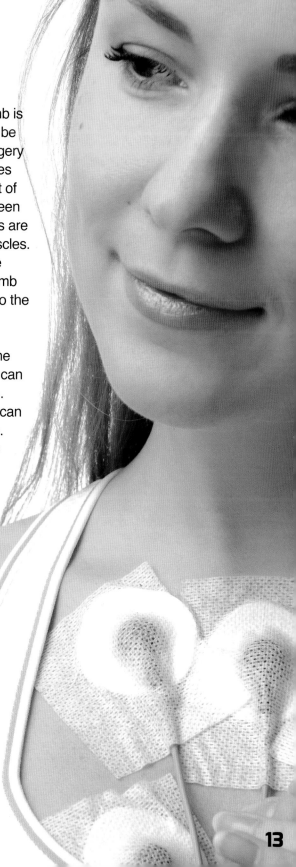

HOW DOES IT WORK?

Before a mind-controlled bionic limb is fitted, a type of **surgery** needs to be performed on the patient. This surgery attaches the patient's broken nerves to a healthy muscle in another part of their body. If a person's arm has been amputated, then the broken nerves are usually attached to their chest muscles. This means that the messages the brain tries to send to the missing limb get looped back around and sent to the patient's chest.

The messages are being sent to the muscle as electric impulses which can then be measured by **electrodes**. By measuring these impulses, we can find out what the brain wants to do. This information is then sent to the bionic prosthetic so it can move exactly how the patient's mind wants it to.

TOUCHING BIONICS

The fact people can now move prosthetic limbs with their minds is truly amazing. It makes the prosthetic feel much more lifelike. But what if bionic limbs could do even more than that? After all, real limbs do more than just move — they also feel.

Our sense of touch is very important to us. You might think of your sense of touch as your ability to feel the **texture** of something, such as the soft fur of a cat or the rough edge of a brick wall. However, our skin can also sense temperature, pressure, pain, and even movement. This is very useful to us. Being able to feel temperature can help to protect us. It tells us to put gloves on when it is too cold outside or to take our hand out from underneath hot running water.

HOW DOES IT WORK?

In the same way we are able to move, we are able to feel because of messages being sent between our bodies and our brains. Our skin has millions of nerve receptors. Different nerve receptors pick up on different things. Some sense temperature, while others sense texture. When you touch something, these receptors send a message to your brain. Messages about what something feels like are carried by sensory neurons. These are different from the motor neurons we looked at earlier whose job it is to control movement.

Some parts of your body have more sensory receptors than others. Your fingertips, for example, have lots. In one square centimeter of your fingertip there are around 2,500 nerve receptors. This makes our hands one of our most important tools for exploring the world around us. This is why it is so important that bionic hands are able to not only move like a real hand, but feel like one too.

YOUR SKIN IS YOUR BODY'S LARGEST ORGAN.

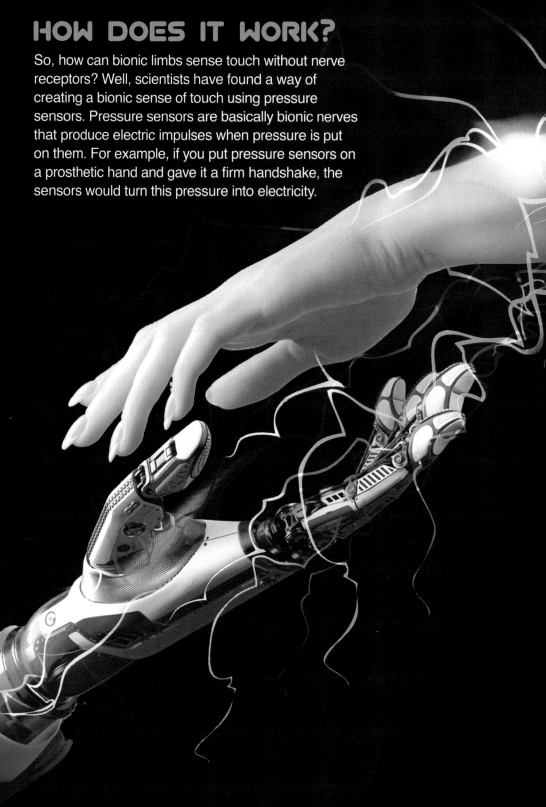

HOW DOES IT WORK?

So, how can bionic limbs sense touch without nerve receptors? Well, scientists have found a way of creating a bionic sense of touch using pressure sensors. Pressure sensors are basically bionic nerves that produce electric impulses when pressure is put on them. For example, if you put pressure sensors on a prosthetic hand and gave it a firm handshake, the sensors would turn this pressure into electricity.

However, for someone to "feel" with a bionic limb, these electric signals must be sent to the patient's brain where they can be understood. Luckily, we already know how to do this. The signals from the pressure sensors can be sent to a computer where they are turned into a specific pattern. This pattern acts like instructions for the brain and is passed on to the nerves in the body using electrodes. This way the brain gets the message sent from the pressure sensors and is able to feel.

Even if bionic limbs could give us superhuman abilities, it would be a shame to lose our sense of touch. We'd never be able to feel another person's hand or feel the sand between our toes when we stand on a beach. This new technology could bring back people's sense of touch and make prosthetics feel much more lifelike.

If we could fit bionic limbs with sensors that could detect heat, texture, pain, and pressure, they might become just as sensitive as real limbs.

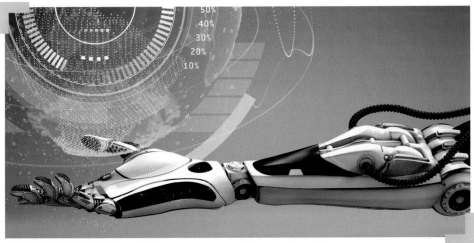

BIONIC SKIN

So, making bionic limbs that can move and feel like real limbs can be done. The next challenge is to make them look like real limbs. After all, even with all the benefits of being part robot, you might not want your limb to stand out. The problem is that it's difficult to make the complicated technology that goes into making a bionic limb look like a real arm or leg.

Some prosthetic arms and legs can be made to look very real. They can be made to match a person's skin tone and some even have hairs and freckles. Unfortunately, these types of prosthetics don't have bionic technology. But, luckily for us, there are scientists out there who are already onto the next step: bionic skin!

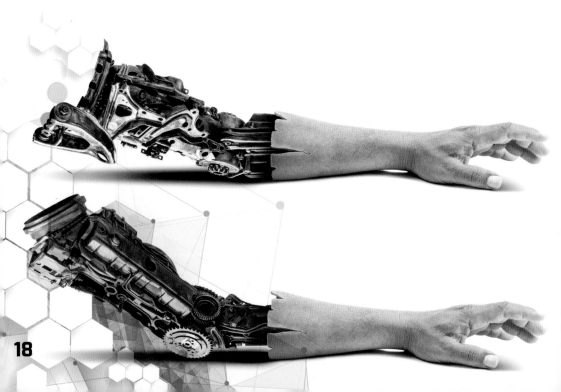

Ideally, bionic skin would look like human skin *and* be able to feel. Scientists have been able to use a 3-D printer to print electronic sensory devices similar to the pressure sensors used to make a feeling bionic limb. 3-D printers work like normal printers but, instead of printing ink, they print many layers of different materials to make a 3-D object.

Scientists believe that these devices could be printed onto artificial skin that is made to look like real skin. It's time to wave goodbye to a future of robots made from metal and held together with nuts and bolts. With artificial skin, a bionic limb and a human limb would look identical!

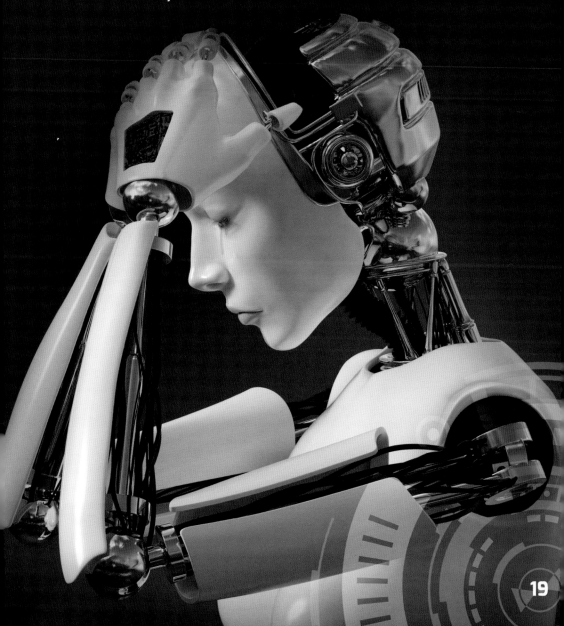

BIONIC SENSES

Bionic limbs can really help people, so why stop there? There are lots of things that can go wrong with our bodies that bionics might be able to fix. The great thing about bionic body parts is that if they go wrong, we can just repair them!

BIONIC EYE

Bionics can help to cure problems that can't be treated with medicine or surgery. For example, many people are born blind or go blind as they get older. Wouldn't it be amazing if bionics could fix our sight if we lost it? It turns out it can! Bionic eyes might mean no one will ever need a pair of glasses again.

To understand how bionic eyes work, we must understand how real eyes work. When light enters our eyes, it hits a part of the eye called the retina. The retina forms an image of what you are seeing and then sends this image to the brain, once again, in the form of electric impulses. Your brain then makes sense of the image and tells you what you are seeing.

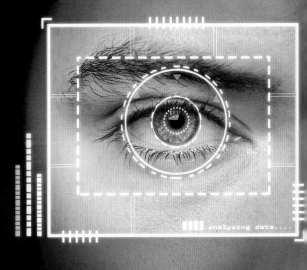

The complicated technology behind a bionic eye begins with two very simple things – a pair of glasses and a video camera. The video camera films the scene in front of you and sends it to a microchip. The microchip turns the images from the camera into patterns of electric signals. These signals are sent to a retina implant in the eye. This implant replaces the real retina, which is often damaged in people who are blind. The retina implant then sends the electric signals to the brain which makes sense of the image!

The bionic eye is not perfect yet. At the moment, it only lets people see in black and white. But it's a promising start for people who would like bionic eyes.

THE WORLD SEEN THROUGH A BIONIC EYE MIGHT LOOK A BIT LIKE THIS:

BIONIC EARS

Not only is it possible to see with bionic eyes, it's also possible to hear with bionic ears. Come again? No, you heard right. Bionic ears are the next step for bionic technology and, luckily, they are much easier to make than bionic eyes. You might think getting a machine to hear sounds would be quite difficult, but actually, it's already being done. Ever searched for something on a phone or computer using your voice? This is called voice recognition, and it works by turning sound waves from your voice into electronic information.

BIONIC EAR

The cochlea is the name given to the inner ear. Just like a retina implant can help a person see, a cochlear implant can help a person to hear if their real cochlea is damaged. Once again, electrodes are used to connect the bionic technology to nerves that carry messages to the brain. Unlike hearing aids, which are only able to make sounds louder, cochlear implants allow you to hear in just three steps:

1. A sound processor picks up on sounds and converts them in to **digital** code.

2. The code is sent to the implant where it's converted into electrical signals.

3. Electrodes send these signals to the brain where the sound is understood.

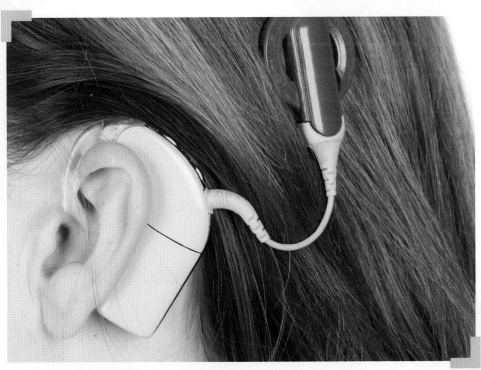

THE HUMAN AND THE MACHINE

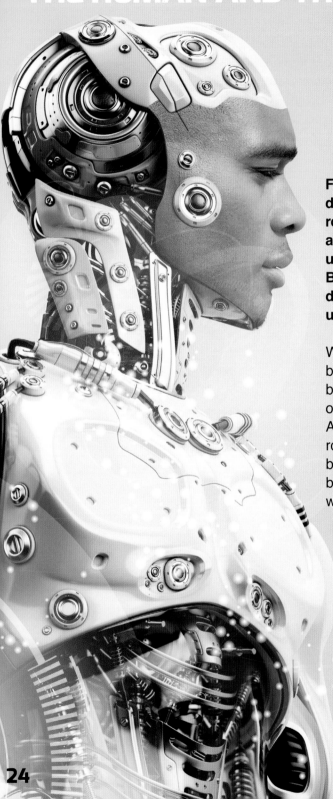

For years, humans have dreamed of building robots that can live alongside us and help us with everyday tasks. But what if robots aren't destined to live alongside us, but *inside* us?

With more and more bionic technology, it might become possible to make ourselves superhuman. After all, who needs robots when you can just become one yourself? If bionics keep improving, who knows what might be next. Bionic limbs with super strength? Eyes with x-ray vision? Ears capable of overhearing conversations from the other side of a crowded room? All these things would give you the skills to become some sort of cyborg secret agent.

REAL-LIFE CYBORGS

NEIL HARBISSON

If you still think cyborgs are a thing of the future, think again. There are already people who have earned the title of cyborg. Take Neil Harbisson for example. He is the first man to be fitted with an antenna. Harbisson is an artist who was born color blind. This means his eyes aren't able to see colors the way most people do.

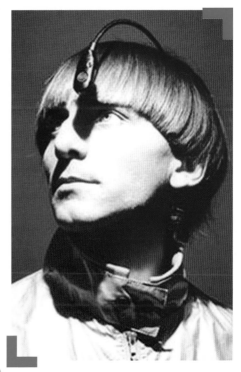

His antenna lets him "hear" colors by turning them into different musical notes. His brain and the antenna have joined together, and now he sees the world completely differently than anybody else.

Harbisson even started the Cyborg Foundation, which is a group that helps people achieve their dream of becoming a cyborg and fights for cyborg rights.

HARBISSON'S ANTENNA ALSO LETS HIM RECEIVE PHONE CALLS THROUGH HIS HEAD!

A B C D E F G

BIONIC BRAINS

Our brains are amazing. They control our bodies and understand the world around us. The brain is where all our thoughts, feelings, and memories come from – our brains make us human. You may have heard people say that our brains are like computers because of the way that they store new information and memories, but what if they really were a computer? Could we make our brains bionic?

A bionic brain would have lots of benefits. Instead of learning new things, you could just download information from the internet straight into your mind. You'd never have to go to school again! By replacing our tired, old brains with better, faster ones, we would truly be welcoming the cyborg life with open (bionic) arms.

Perhaps a super-intelligent, fully bionic brain belongs more to the world of science fiction than of science fact. However, scientists really are working on making parts of our brains bionic. They have discovered ways to use microchips to reconnect parts of the brain that have become damaged.

Sometimes head injuries can cause people to become paralyzed. This means they can't move certain parts of their bodies at all. Scientists hope that microchips can repair broken connections in the brain. For someone who is paralyzed, this might help messages from the brain reach the parts of their bodies that they are unable to move. Microchips would be like bionic limbs for the brain!

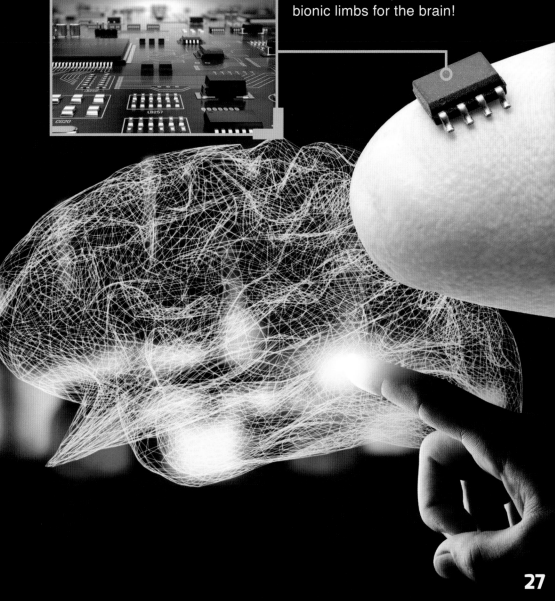

BIONICS:
THE FUTURE

The world of bionics is moving fast, but is it all as good as it seems? Bionic brains might be great. Instead of studying for a test, we could simply download the correct answers straight to our minds. We might even be able to download and share our memories or record our dreams and watch them back.

But, what if our bionic brains went wrong? What would happen then? Our brains keep us alive for years and years, but computers often break down. What if you're in the middle of a test and your bionic brain crashes and loses all its memories? Even more worryingly, if our brains are like computers, they could be hacked. If our thoughts and feelings are stored in bionic brains, people might be able to hack into our brains and read our minds!

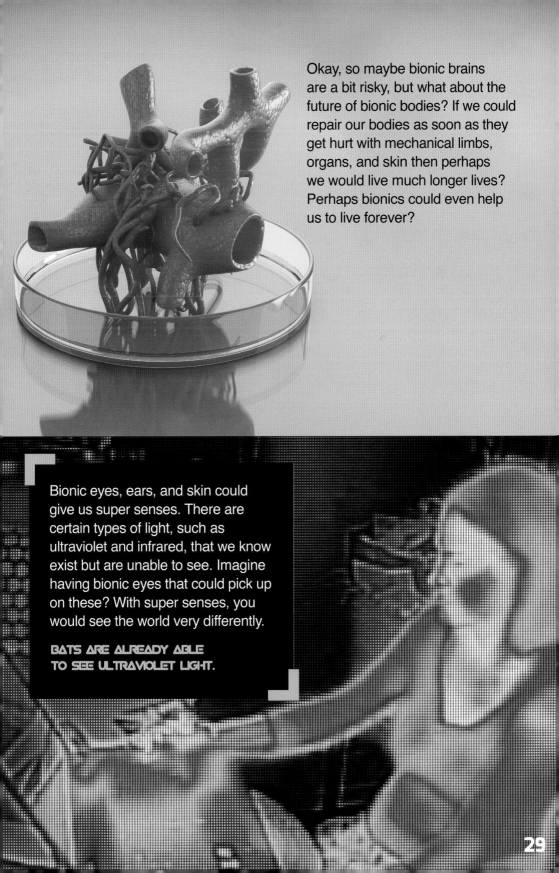

Okay, so maybe bionic brains are a bit risky, but what about the future of bionic bodies? If we could repair our bodies as soon as they get hurt with mechanical limbs, organs, and skin then perhaps we would live much longer lives? Perhaps bionics could even help us to live forever?

Bionic eyes, ears, and skin could give us super senses. There are certain types of light, such as ultraviolet and infrared, that we know exist but are unable to see. Imagine having bionic eyes that could pick up on these? With super senses, you would see the world very differently.

BATS ARE ALREADY ABLE TO SEE ULTRAVIOLET LIGHT.

DUE FOR AN UPGRADE?

If it gave you superstrength, super senses, and super intelligence, would you upgrade your human body and become a cyborg? It might not be long before everyone is after the latest cybernetic enhancement. Before you know it, you might have a cyborg teacher with bionic eyes in the back of their head!

Bionics can be really helpful for people with disabilities. What else do you see in the future of bionics? Can you imagine a world where everyone wants to become part robot? Would we lose what makes us human – our memories, our emotions, or our individuality – and turn ourselves into a race of unfeeling robots like the Cybermen? If this has sparked your imagination, why not try writing some science fiction of your own? Who knows? One day it might be science fact.

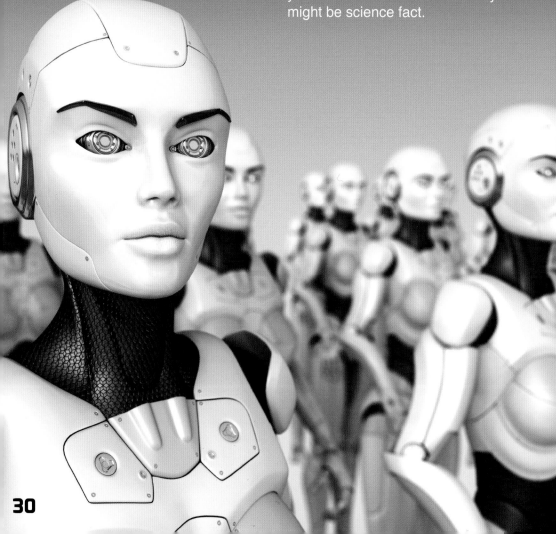

GLOSSARY

3-D	an object which has height, width, and depth
amputated	cut off in a surgical operation
antenna	a long, thin sensor, usually found on the heads of insects
artificial	made by humans
automatic	works without conscious thought or control
biology	the study of the body and how it works
blind	unable to see
cells	the basic units that make up all living things
digital	information that is expressed as a series of the digits 0 and 1
electrodes	electric conductors used to transfer electricity to nonconductive materials
engineers	people who design and build machines
hacked	to have information or data stolen
implant	an object that has been inserted into the body
impulses	a brief pulse of electrical energy
mechanical	operated by a machine
microchip	a very small piece of material holding a group of tiny electronic circuits.
organ	a (self-contained) part of a living thing that has a specific, important function
surgery	the treatment of injuries and diseases through operations
technology	machines or devices that are made using scientific knowledge
texture	the tactile feel of something

INDEX